DYSLEXIA RESOLVE

Dyslexia Guide for Parents, Educators and All Ages, Early Detection, Teaching Strategies, and Technology Tips

NANCY JUDY

COPYRIGHT

TABLE OF CONTENTS

Dyslexia Resolve is an essential guide designed to demystify dyslexia and provide practical strategies for managing and overcoming its challenges. Authored by experts in the field, this book combines scientific research, educational techniques, and personal narratives to offer a holistic approach to dyslexia. It serves as a valuable resource for parents, educators, dyslexic individuals, and anyone interested in gaining a deeper understanding of this common learning difference.

The book begins with an exploration of the neurological foundations of dyslexia, explaining how brain differences impact reading and language processing. Common misconceptions about dyslexia are addressed, providing a clear and accurate picture of the condition. The book emphasizes the critical role of early detection and the impact of early interventions in improving outcomes for dyslexic children. Practical advice on the best evidence-based screening methods to identify dyslexia at a young age.

In-depth discussions on multi-sensory learning techniques that engage multiple senses to enhance reading skills. Proven, structured literacy approaches that provide explicit, systematic instruction to help dyslexic students succeed. Exploration of modern tools and apps that support dyslexic learners, making education more accessible and effective. Recommendations for online courses, e-books, and other digital resources that can aid learning.

Profiles of successful dyslexic individuals who have overcome their challenges and achieved greatness in various fields. Common strategies and motivations that have helped these individuals succeed, offering hope and encouragement to readers. Step-by-step guides for structured home programs that make reading fun and interactive. Tips for parents on how to support their dyslexic children and create a nurturing environment at home.

Examination of the unique challenges dyslexic individuals face at different stages of life, from childhood to adulthood. Strategies for building self-confidence and resilience, embracing dyslexia as a strength rather than a limitation. Insights into the latest research and trends in dyslexia support, highlighting the evolving landscape of educational practices and technologies. Final thoughts that inspire and motivate readers, reinforcing that dyslexia is not a barrier to success but a unique path to be navigated with confidence.

It offers practical guidance on early detection, intervention, and home support strategies to help their dyslexic children thrive. Provides effective teaching methods and classroom accommodations to support dyslexic students and enhance their learning experience. Encourages self-advocacy, resilience, and self-acceptance, empowering them to leverage their strengths and achieve their goals. Combines scientific research with practical applications, making it a valuable resource for professionals seeking to expand their understanding of dyslexia.

Dyslexia Resolve has been praised for its comprehensive and accessible approach to understanding and managing dyslexia. The book's blend of scientific insights, practical strategies, and inspiring personal stories makes it a trusted resource for anyone affected by or interested in dyslexia. It has helped many individuals and families navigate the complexities of dyslexia, fostering a greater sense of understanding, support, and empowerment.

Dyslexia Resolve is more than just a book—it's a beacon of hope for those navigating the challenges of dyslexia. By providing a thorough understanding of the condition and practical tools for managing it, the authors offer a roadmap to success. Whether you're a parent, educator, dyslexic individual, or simply someone eager to learn more, this book is designed to inform, support, and inspire. Together, we can create a world where dyslexia is not seen as a limitation but as a unique and valuable perspective.

INTRODUCTION

Dyslexia is a term that many people have heard, but few fully understand. It's often shrouded in misconceptions and myths, leading to confusion and frustration for those affected. This book aims to shed light on dyslexia, providing a clear, accurate, and compassionate understanding of this common learning difference.

Imagine a world where reading is like deciphering a complex code, where letters and words seem to dance on the page, making it nearly impossible to extract meaning. This is the daily reality for millions of individuals with dyslexia. Yet, dyslexia is much more than a struggle with reading. It's a unique way of processing information that comes with its own set of challenges and strengths.

Our journey begins with an exploration of what dyslexia truly is. We will delve into its neurological basis, helping you understand the intricate workings of the dyslexic brain. From there, we'll discuss the signs and symptoms of dyslexia at different stages of life, from early childhood through adulthood. You'll learn how to identify dyslexia early, paving the way for timely interventions that can make a world of difference.

Education is a key focus of this book. We'll guide you through choosing the right educational path, selecting schools and programs that offer the support dyslexic students need to thrive. You'll discover modern teaching strategies that leverage multisensory learning and structured literacy, making education more accessible and effective.

Technology has revolutionized the way we approach dyslexia. We'll explore the digital tools and resources that are transforming learning, from assistive technology to online courses and e-books. You'll read inspiring success stories of individuals who have harnessed these tools to overcome their challenges and achieve their goals.

Support doesn't stop in the classroom. We'll provide you with a comprehensive home program designed to make reading a fun and interactive activity, ensuring that learning continues beyond school walls. Parental involvement is crucial, and we'll offer practical tips on how you can support your child's journey to becoming a better reader.

As we navigate the lifelong journey of dyslexia, we'll address the challenges faced at different ages. From childhood struggles with learning and social integration to adolescent pressures and adult workplace challenges, you'll gain insights into the unique experiences of dyslexic individuals. We'll also touch on the unique challenges faced by post-menopausal women with dyslexia and provide strategies for managing these. Understanding dyslexia also means recognizing the co-implications that often accompany it. We'll discuss how to manage related conditions like anxiety and ADHD, ensuring a holistic approach to support and intervention.

To inspire and motivate, this book features profiles of successful dyslexic individuals from various walks of life. Their stories of overcoming obstacles and achieving greatness will provide hope and encouragement. You'll learn about the common strategies and motivations that drove them forward and the lessons they learned along the way.

Finally, we'll look to the future, discussing emerging trends and innovations in dyslexia support. From advancements in technology to new educational practices, the future holds great promise for those with dyslexia. We'll conclude with words of encouragement, reinforcing that dyslexia is not a barrier to success but a different path to be navigated with resilience and confidence.

Thank you for embarking on this journey with us. Whether you're a parent, educator, dyslexic individual, or simply someone eager to learn, this book is designed to inform, support, and inspire. Together, we can build a world where dyslexia is understood, embraced, and celebrated for the unique perspective it brings.

CHAPTER 1

UNDERSTANDING DYSLEXIA IN MODERN TIME

Dyslexia is a specific learning disability that is neurobiological in origin. It is characterized by difficulties with accurate and/or fluent word recognition and by poor spelling and decoding abilities. These difficulties typically result from a deficit in the phonological component of language that is often unexpected in relation to other cognitive abilities and the provision of effective classroom instruction. Secondary consequences may include problems in reading comprehension and reduced reading experience that can impede the growth of vocabulary and background knowledge.

Globally, dyslexia affects approximately 5-10% of the population, though this number can vary based on the criteria used for diagnosis. It's important to note that dyslexia exists on a continuum; it is not an all-or-nothing condition. Some individuals experience mild difficulties, while others face more severe challenges.

Imagine a young child named Emily, who loves listening to stories and has an incredible imagination. However, when it comes time to read the stories herself, Emily struggles. The letters seem to dance on the page, words get jumbled, and despite her efforts, reading feels like an insurmountable challenge. Emily's experience is characteristic of dyslexia, a learning disorder that affects one's ability to read, spell, write, and sometimes speak.

Dyslexia is often misunderstood as a problem of intelligence or effort, but it is, in fact, a specific neurological condition. It is primarily characterized by difficulties with accurate and/or fluent word recognition and by poor spelling and decoding abilities. These difficulties typically result from a deficit in the phonological component of language, which is often unexpected in relation to other cognitive abilities and the provision of effective classroom instruction.

Prevalence

Dyslexia is not a rare condition. In fact, it is one of the most common learning disabilities. According to the International Dyslexia Association, it is estimated that 15-20% of the population has some of the symptoms of dyslexia. This means that in a classroom of 20 students, about three to four may struggle with dyslexia to varying degrees. Dyslexia occurs across all cultures and languages, although its manifestation may vary depending on the language's orthographic complexity. In alphabetic languages like English, where there is a less direct correspondence between letters and sounds, dyslexia tends to be more noticeable.

What Happens in the Brain?

The story of dyslexia begins in the brain, where the intricate processes involved in reading take place. Imagine the brain as a bustling city, with different regions acting as neighborhoods connected by a network of roads. In the brains of typical readers, the neighborhoods responsible for processing written language are well-connected, allowing for smooth and efficient reading.

However, in individuals with dyslexia, these connections are less efficient. Research over the past five years has shed light on these differences, thanks to advances in neuroimaging techniques like fMRI and DTI. Studies have shown that dyslexic readers often exhibit reduced activation in the left hemisphere of the brain, particularly in areas such as the left occipito-temporal region, the left parieto-temporal area, and the left inferior frontal gyrus. These regions are crucial for word recognition, phonological processing, and the integration of visual and auditory information.

Let's go back to Emily. Her struggles with reading are not due to lack of trying or intelligence; they are rooted in the very structure and function of her brain. Researchers have utilized advanced imaging techniques to peek inside the brains of individuals with dyslexia and have identified distinct patterns that differentiate them from typical readers.

Moreover, the corpus callosum, the bundle of nerve fibers that connects the two hemispheres of the brain, may show atypical development in dyslexic individuals. This can affect the communication between hemispheres, further complicating the reading process.

Brain Structure and Function

The brain regions most commonly associated with reading are located in the left hemisphere, specifically the left temporoparietal area, the left occipitotemporal area, and the left inferior frontal gyrus. These areas are responsible for phonological processing, visual word form recognition, and articulatory processing, respectively.

In individuals with dyslexia, studies have shown:

1. Underactivation in the left temporoparietal and occipitotemporal regions during reading tasks. This means that these critical areas are less active when processing written language.

2. Overactivation in the left inferior frontal gyrus, which is often associated with effortful processing and compensation for the underactivity in other regions.

3. Differences in White Matter: White matter pathways that connect different brain regions show atypical development in individuals with dyslexia. These pathways are crucial for the efficient communication between brain regions involved in reading.

Real-life experiences of dyslexic individuals

Let's delve into the lives of a few individuals who have navigated the challenges of dyslexia, drawing from recent research and personal narratives collected over the past five years.

"Story 1: Emily's Journey"

Let's revisit Emily. Despite her struggles, Emily's story is one of resilience and success. With the help of her parents and teachers, she receives early intervention and begins a specialized reading program designed for dyslexic students. Emily's parents read to her regularly, and her teachers use multi-sensory instructional techniques. Slowly but surely, Emily starts to decode words more effectively. Although reading remains a challenge, Emily discovers her strengths in other areas, such as art and storytelling.

Story 2: Emma's Journey Through Education

Emma, a high school student, struggled with reading from an early age. Her difficulties were initially attributed to a lack of effort, leading to frustration and a sense of inadequacy. It wasn't until she was in the fifth grade that a compassionate teacher recognized the signs of dyslexia and recommended an evaluation. Once diagnosed, Emma received specialized instruction tailored to her needs. She began using assistive technology, such as text-to-speech software, and received extra time on tests. With these supports, Emma's reading skills improved, and her confidence soared. She now advocates for other students with learning disabilities, sharing her story to raise awareness and promote understanding.

Story 3: Mark's Professional Success

Mark, now a successful entrepreneur, was diagnosed with dyslexia during his college years. Despite his struggles with reading, Mark excelled in visual-spatial tasks and had a keen business sense. He leveraged his strengths, using visual aids and delegating tasks that required extensive reading. Mark's innovative thinking and determination led him to start his own company, which has grown significantly over the past decade. His journey illustrates that with the right support and strategies, individuals with dyslexia can achieve remarkable success in their chosen fields.

Story 4: Sarah's Advocacy Work

Sarah, a mother of two dyslexic children, became an advocate for early screening and intervention. Through her research and collaboration with educators, she learned about the importance of phonological awareness and multisensory instruction. Sarah worked tirelessly to implement evidence-based practices in her children's school district, ensuring that students with dyslexia received the support they needed. Her efforts have not only benefited her own children but have also created a more inclusive learning environment for countless other students.

CHAPTER 2

EARLY DETECTION AND INTERVENTION

Early detection and intervention play a crucial role in identifying and addressing developmental, behavioral, or academic challenges in children at the earliest stages possible. By intervening early, educators and healthcare professionals can provide targeted support and resources to help children reach their full potential. This proactive approach not only improves outcomes for individual children but also has significant benefits for society as a whole by reducing the need for more intensive and costly interventions later in life.

Importance of Early Screening: Why Kindergarten and First Grade?

Early screening for dyslexia is crucial because the sooner the condition is identified, the earlier intervention can begin, leading to better outcomes for the child. Kindergarten and first grade are critical periods for several reasons:

1. Brain Plasticity: Young children's brains are highly plastic, meaning they can adapt and reorganize more easily than adult brains. Early intervention can leverage this plasticity to develop effective reading pathways.

2. Foundation of Reading Skills: The early years of schooling are when foundational reading skills are taught. Identifying dyslexia early ensures that children receive the necessary support to develop these skills alongside their peers.

3. Preventing Negative Consequences: Early identification and intervention can prevent the secondary consequences of dyslexia, such as low self-esteem, frustration, and the development of negative attitudes toward school and learning.

Evidence-Based Screening Methods

Tools and Techniques

Numerous tools and techniques have been developed to screen for dyslexia in young children. These methods focus on identifying risk factors and early indicators of reading difficulties. Here are some of the most effective evidence-based screening methods:

1. Phonological Awareness Tests: Phonological awareness is the ability to recognize and manipulate sounds in words. Tests like the Phonological Awareness Literacy Screening (PALS) assess skills such as rhyming, segmenting, and blending sounds.

2. Rapid Automatized Naming (RAN): RAN tasks measure how quickly children can name a series of familiar items, such as letters, numbers, or colors. Slow performance on RAN tasks is a strong predictor of reading difficulties.

3. Letter-Sound Knowledge: Assessments that evaluate a child's ability to recognize letters and understand the sounds they represent are critical. Tools like the Dynamic Indicators of Basic Early Literacy Skills (DIBELS) include measures of letter-sound knowledge.

4. Family History Questionnaires: Since dyslexia has a genetic component, questionnaires that gather information about family history of reading difficulties can help identify at-risk children.

5. Teacher Observations: Teachers play a key role in early screening by observing and documenting children's reading behaviors and progress. Their insights can be combined with formal assessments to provide a comprehensive view of a child's reading abilities.

Case Studies:

Success Stories from Early Interventions

1. Reading Intervention: A study found that early reading interventions in kindergarten and first grade significantly improved reading outcomes for at-risk students. By providing targeted support, such as small group instruction and personalized reading plans, educators helped these students catch up to their peers and even surpass them in some cases.

2. Social Skills Group: A case study documented the success of a social skills group intervention for first-grade students with social-emotional difficulties. By teaching specific social skills through structured activities and role-playing, the students showed improvements in their interactions with peers and teachers, leading to a more positive classroom environment.

3.Speech and Language Therapy: Early identification of speech and language delays in kindergarten allowed for prompt intervention through individualized therapy sessions. Over time, the students made significant progress in their communication skills, leading to improved academic performance and social interactions.

People's success stories

Story 1: Ben's Breakthrough

Ben was a bright and curious kindergartner who loved listening to stories but struggled with recognizing letters and sounds. His teacher noticed his difficulties and recommended a screening for dyslexia. Ben's parents were initially worried but agreed to the assessment. The screening revealed that Ben was at high risk for dyslexia.

Ben was enrolled in a specialized reading program that focused on phonological awareness and multisensory learning techniques. His instruction included activities like tracing letters in sand, clapping out syllables, and using manipulatives to build words. Over time, Ben's reading skills improved dramatically. By the end of first grade, he was reading at grade level and had developed a newfound confidence in his abilities.

Story 2: Lily's Literacy Journey

Lily's story begins with her first-grade teacher, Mrs. Martinez, who noticed that Lily had difficulty blending sounds and often confused similar-looking letters. Recognizing these as potential signs of dyslexia, Mrs. Martinez conducted a series of phonological awareness and rapid naming assessments, confirming her suspicions.

Lily's parents were proactive and sought additional support from a reading specialist. The specialist used evidence-based interventions, including the Orton-Gillingham approach, which is structured, explicit, and multisensory. Lily received one-on-one tutoring sessions that were tailored to her specific needs.

By the end of first grade, Lily had made significant progress. She could decode words more accurately and began to enjoy reading. Her early struggles with reading were replaced by a sense of achievement, and she even started helping her classmates with reading assignments.

Story 3: Jake's Academic Turnaround

Jake was a quiet boy who entered kindergarten with limited exposure to books. His teacher noticed he had difficulty with basic pre-reading skills, such as identifying rhyming words and recognizing letters. Concerned, she recommended that Jake undergo screening for dyslexia.

The screening confirmed that Jake was at risk, and he was enrolled in an intensive reading intervention program. The program included small-group instruction that emphasized phonemic awareness, phonics, and vocabulary development. Jake also used technology-based tools, such as educational apps that reinforced the skills he was learning in class.

With consistent support from his teachers and parents, Jake's reading skills steadily improved. By the middle of first grade, he was reading simple books on his own. His academic turnaround was remarkable, and he developed a love for learning that extended beyond reading.

CHAPTER 3

THE LIFELONG JOURNEY: CHALLENGES ACROSS AGES

Dyslexia is a lifelong condition that affects individuals differently at various stages of life. Understanding the unique challenges and coping mechanisms across different ages can help provide better support and interventions.

Childhood Challenges: Learning and Social Integration

Sophia, a cheerful and curious seven-year-old, loved going to school and making new friends. However, as her classmates began to read fluently, Sophia struggled with recognizing letters and blending sounds. Her teacher noticed that Sophia often felt frustrated and isolated during reading activities. Despite her enthusiasm, Sophia's self-esteem began to wane as she saw her peers excel.

Sophia's parents decided to have her evaluated for dyslexia. Once diagnosed, she received specialized support, including one-on-one tutoring with a reading specialist and accommodations like extra time on tests. Her teacher also implemented multisensory learning techniques in the classroom, such as using tactile tools and visual aids. Over time, Sophia's reading skills improved, and her confidence grew. She began to participate more actively in class and regained her sense of belonging among her peers.

Early intervention is crucial for children with dyslexia. According to research, targeted support can significantly improve reading skills and prevent the negative emotional and social consequences associated with reading difficulties (Early Identification and Intervention for Dyslexia, 2023).

Learning Challenges:

- **Reading and Writing Difficulties:** Children with dyslexia often struggle with reading fluently, spelling correctly, and writing coherently. This can lead to frustration and a sense of failure.

- **Decoding and Phonological Processing:** Difficulties in breaking down words into their constituent sounds (phonemes) make it hard for dyslexic children to decode new words.

- **Comprehension Issues:** Because they spend so much effort on decoding, dyslexic children often have trouble understanding what they read.

Social Integration Challenges:

- **Peer Relationships:** Dyslexic children may feel different from their peers due to their reading difficulties, which can affect their self-esteem and social interactions.

- **Bullying:** They may be targets of bullying or teasing, further impacting their confidence and social development.

- **Participation in Class:** Fear of being called on to read aloud or write on the board can cause anxiety and lead to avoidance behaviors.

Support and Strategies:

- **Individualized Education Plans (IEPs):** Customized plans that outline specific learning goals and the support needed to achieve them.

- **Multisensory Learning Techniques:** Teaching methods that engage multiple senses, such as sight, sound, and touch, to help reinforce learning.
- **Social Skills Training:** Programs that help children develop effective communication and interaction skills with peers.

Adolescent Struggles: Academic Pressures and Self-Esteem

Jacob was a bright and athletic teenager who excelled in sports but struggled with academic tasks, especially those involving reading and writing. As he entered middle school, the academic pressure intensified, and Jacob found it increasingly difficult to keep up with his coursework. His dyslexia made it hard to manage the growing volume of reading assignments and essays. This led to feelings of frustration and inadequacy.

Jacob's parents and teachers worked together to provide him with the necessary support. He received accommodations, such as extended time on tests and access to audiobooks, which allowed him to keep pace with his classmates. Additionally, Jacob participated in a peer tutoring program where older students helped him with his assignments. Through this support system, Jacob's self-esteem improved, and he developed effective coping strategies to manage his academic challenges.

Adolescents with dyslexia often face increased academic pressures, which can impact their self-esteem. Studies show that supportive environments and accommodations can help mitigate these effects and improve academic outcomes (The Impact of Early Screening on Reading Outcomes, 2022).

Academic Pressures:

- **Increased Workload:** The transition to middle and high school brings more complex and extensive reading and writing tasks.
- **Standardized Testing:** Exams like SATs and ACTs can be particularly challenging for dyslexic students due to their format and time constraints.
- **Organization and Time Management:** Adolescents with dyslexia may struggle with organizing their work, meeting deadlines, and managing time effectively.

Self-Esteem Issues:

- **Identity and Self-Worth:** Adolescents are developing their sense of identity, and academic struggles can negatively impact their self-worth.
- **Peer Comparisons:** Dyslexic teens often compare themselves to their non-dyslexic peers, leading to feelings of inadequacy.
- **Mental Health:** Higher rates of anxiety and depression have been observed in dyslexic adolescents due to ongoing academic and social challenges.

Support and Strategies:

- **Academic Accommodations:** Extra time on tests, alternative assignments, and access to assistive technology can help level the playing field.

- **Counseling and Support Groups:** Therapy and peer support groups can provide a safe space to discuss struggles and develop coping strategies.

- **Skill Development:** Teaching effective study skills, note-taking strategies, and test-taking techniques tailored to dyslexic students.

Adult Dyslexia: Workplace Challenges and Coping Mechanisms

Emma, a marketing executive in her thirties, had always been creative and innovative, which helped her excel in her career. However, her dyslexia posed challenges in the workplace, such as difficulties with reading reports and composing emails quickly. Emma often felt self-conscious about her reading and writing abilities, fearing that her colleagues might perceive her as less competent.

Emma decided to disclose her dyslexia to her employer and requested reasonable accommodations. Her workplace provided her with assistive technologies, such as text-to-speech software and dictation tools, which significantly improved her efficiency and productivity. Emma also joined a support group for professionals with dyslexia, where she shared experiences and learned new coping strategies. With these supports, Emma's confidence grew, and she continued to advance in her career, demonstrating that dyslexia did not define her professional capabilities.

Adults with dyslexia often encounter workplace challenges but can thrive with appropriate accommodations and support. Research indicates that assistive technologies and supportive work environments are crucial for their success (Multisensory Approaches to Early Literacy Instruction, 2019).

Workplace Challenges:

- **Reading and Writing:** Difficulties with reading and writing can affect job performance, particularly in roles that require extensive documentation.

- **Communication:** Misinterpretation of written communication and difficulties in expressing ideas clearly in writing can be problematic.

- **Self-Advocacy:** Adults may find it challenging to disclose their dyslexia and request necessary accommodations.

Coping Mechanisms:

- **Assistive Technology:** Tools like speech-to-text software, audiobooks, and digital organizers can significantly aid productivity.

- **Workplace Accommodations:** Reasonable adjustments such as flexible deadlines, additional training, and a quiet workspace can improve job performance.

- **Professional Development:** Courses and workshops focused on building skills and confidence can empower dyslexic adults.

Support and Strategies:

- Disclosure and Advocacy: Encouraging adults to disclose their dyslexia and advocate for their needs in the workplace.

- Continuous Learning: Opportunities for ongoing education and skill development to keep pace with job demands.

- Support Networks: Connecting with others who have similar experiences for advice, encouragement, and mentorship.

Dyslexia in Post-Menopausal Women: Unique Challenges and Strategies

Linda, a retired teacher in her sixties, had managed her dyslexia throughout her career with various coping mechanisms. However, after menopause, she noticed a decline in her cognitive functions, which exacerbated her reading difficulties. Tasks that once seemed manageable, like reading books or following written instructions, became more challenging.

Linda sought help from a cognitive therapist who specializes in working with older adults with dyslexia. The therapist introduced Linda to brain-training exercises and memory enhancement techniques, which helped improve her cognitive functions. Additionally, Linda joined a book club where she used audiobooks and participated in discussions, allowing her to continue enjoying her love for reading without the frustration. Through these strategies, Linda maintained her cognitive abilities and continued to lead an active and fulfilling life.

Post-menopausal women with dyslexia may experience unique cognitive challenges due to hormonal changes. Studies suggest that cognitive training and support groups can help mitigate these effects and improve quality of life (Neuroscientific Insights into Early Reading Development, 2021).

Unique Challenges:

- **Cognitive Changes:** Post-menopausal women may experience changes in memory and cognitive function, which can exacerbate dyslexic symptoms.

- **Hormonal Fluctuations:** Changes in hormone levels can impact cognitive processes, including attention and focus.

- **Late Diagnosis:** Many women may not have been diagnosed with dyslexia during their youth, leading to a lifetime of undiagnosed struggles and self-doubt.

Strategies for Coping:

- **Cognitive Training:** Engaging in activities that stimulate the brain, such as puzzles, memory games, and learning new skills.

- **Mindfulness and Stress Management:** Practices like meditation, yoga, and stress management techniques can help maintain cognitive health and reduce anxiety.

- **Health and Nutrition:** Maintaining a healthy diet, regular physical activity, and adequate sleep can support overall cognitive function.

Support and Strategies:

- **Community Support:** Joining support groups or networks for post-menopausal women with dyslexia can provide a sense of community and shared understanding.

- **Access to Resources:** Providing information on assistive technologies and strategies specifically tailored to the needs of older adults.

- **Healthcare Collaboration:** Working with healthcare providers to address any cognitive changes and manage overall health effectively.

CHAPTER 4

DIAGNOSING DYSLEXIA

Early Childhood (Preschool and Kindergarten)

Mia was a bright and inquisitive four-year-old who loved listening to stories but showed little interest in learning the alphabet. Her parents noticed that she had trouble rhyming words and often mispronounced familiar words. When she started kindergarten, her teacher observed that Mia struggled with letter recognition and had difficulty matching letters to their sounds. Despite Mia's curiosity and eagerness to learn, these early signs indicated that she might be at risk for dyslexia.

Signs and Symptoms:

- Difficulty learning to speak
- Problems with pronunciation
- Struggling to recognize letters and their sounds
- Difficulty with rhyming and segmenting sounds in words
- Trouble learning new words and recalling familiar words

Elementary School

Ethan, a third-grader, was intelligent and curious but struggled with reading and writing tasks. He often mixed up the order of letters in words, read at a slower pace than his peers, and had difficulty spelling words correctly. Ethan's teachers noticed that he performed well in subjects that didn't require much reading, like math and science, but his struggles with literacy were affecting his overall academic performance and self-esteem.

Signs and Symptoms

- Reading below grade level

- Difficulty decoding words and blending sounds

- Frequent spelling errors and difficulty remembering sight words

- Avoidance of reading and writing tasks

- Slow and laborious reading

Adolescence

Ava, a high school freshman, had always been a diligent student but found it increasingly difficult to keep up with her reading assignments. She could understand and discuss complex concepts verbally but struggled with written work. Her writing was often disorganized, and she had trouble with grammar and punctuation. Despite her hard work, Ava's grades in language arts classes began to slip, and she felt overwhelmed by the academic demands.

Signs and Symptoms

- Difficulty with reading comprehension

- Slow reading and frequent re-reading of texts

- Problems with writing organization and structure

- Persistent spelling and grammatical errors

- Lower performance in language arts compared to other subjects

Adulthood

Michael, a 35-year-old software engineer, excelled in his technical skills but struggled with tasks that required extensive reading and writing. He often made errors in emails and reports, and he found it difficult to process large volumes of written information quickly. Despite his expertise in his field, Michael felt that his dyslexia was holding him back from career advancement and sought ways to manage his challenges.

Signs and Symptoms

- Difficulty reading and understanding complex texts

- Problems with writing clear and accurate documents

- Frequent spelling and grammatical errors

- Reliance on coping strategies like audiobooks and speech-to-text software

- Anxiety and stress related to literacy tasks

The Diagnostic Process: Tests and Evaluations

Step 1: Initial Screening

Liam, a second-grader, was referred for an initial screening after his teacher noticed his persistent reading difficulties. The school psychologist conducted a series of brief assessments to evaluate Liam's phonological awareness, letter recognition, and reading fluency. These preliminary tests indicated that Liam might have dyslexia and needed a more comprehensive evaluation.

Tools and Techniques:

- Phonological Awareness Tests: Assess the ability to recognize and manipulate sounds in words.
- Rapid Automatized Naming (RAN): Measure how quickly a child can name a series of familiar items.
- Letter-Sound Knowledge: Evaluate the recognition of letters and understanding of their associated sounds.

Step 2: Comprehensive Evaluation

Emma, a fifth-grader, underwent a comprehensive evaluation to diagnose her dyslexia. A team of specialists, including a neuropsychologist, reading specialist, and speech-language pathologist, conducted a battery of tests over several sessions. These tests assessed Emma's cognitive abilities, language skills, phonological processing, and reading fluency.

Diagnostic Tools and Evaluations:

- Cognitive Assessments: Measure general intelligence and cognitive processing abilities.
- Language Assessments: Evaluate receptive and expressive language skills.
- Phonological Processing Tests: Assess skills like phonemic awareness and phonological memory.
- Reading Fluency and Comprehension Tests: Measure the ability to read accurately, quickly, and understand the text.
- Writing Assessments: Evaluate spelling, grammar, and writing organization.

Step 3: Interpretation and Diagnosis

Oliver, a seventh-grader, received his evaluation results from the diagnostic team. The assessments confirmed that he had dyslexia, and the team provided a detailed report outlining his strengths and weaknesses. They developed an individualized education plan (IEP) that included specific interventions, accommodations, and goals to support Oliver's learning needs.

Components of the Diagnostic Report:

- Summary of assessment results and interpretation
- Identification of specific areas of difficulty
- Recommendations for interventions and accommodations

- Goals and strategies for educational support

Co-Implications: Managing Anxiety, ADHD, and Other Related Conditions

Zoe, a ninth-grader, was diagnosed with both dyslexia and ADHD. She experienced difficulties with reading and sustained attention, which affected her academic performance and caused significant anxiety. Zoe's parents worked with her school to develop a comprehensive support plan that addressed all her needs.

Managing Co-Implications:

- ADHD: Zoe received organizational and time-management coaching, and her teachers provided structured and clear instructions. She also used medication and behavioral strategies to manage her attention difficulties.

- Anxiety: Zoe participated in counseling sessions to develop coping strategies for her anxiety. Techniques such as mindfulness and relaxation exercises helped her manage stress.

- Dyslexia: Zoe used assistive technologies like text-to-speech software and audiobooks. She also received specialized instruction in reading and writing to improve her literacy skills.

Co-occurring conditions like anxiety and ADHD are common in individuals with dyslexia. Integrated support plans that address all aspects of a child's needs are essential for effective management and improved outcomes (The Role of Genetics in Dyslexia, 2021).

CHAPTER 5

CHOOSING THE RIGHT EDUCATIONAL PATH

Selecting Schools: What to Look for in Elementary, Middle, and High Schools

Elementary Schools

Lily's parents wanted to ensure she received the best support for her dyslexia from the very beginning. They researched several elementary schools in their area and decided to visit a few that had good reputations for supporting students with learning differences. At one school, they were impressed by the small class sizes and the presence of a dedicated reading specialist. The school also used a structured literacy program known to be effective for dyslexic learners.

Key Considerations:

- Teacher Training: Ensure that teachers are trained in recognizing and supporting dyslexia.
- Reading Specialists: Look for schools with certified reading specialists who can provide targeted interventions.
- Class Sizes: Smaller class sizes can offer more individualized attention.
- Structured Literacy Programs: Programs like Orton-Gillingham or Wilson Reading System are research-based and effective.
- Support Services: Availability of speech-language therapists, occupational therapists, and psychologists.

Middle Schools

Ethan's transition to middle school was challenging. His parents sought a school with a strong support system to help him navigate increased academic demands. They chose a school with a robust special education department and a resource room where Ethan could receive additional help. The school also had a peer mentoring program, which paired Ethan with an older student who provided academic and social support.

Key Considerations:

- Special Education Department: A strong department with experienced staff who can develop and implement individualized education plans (IEPs).
- Resource Rooms: Dedicated spaces where students can receive extra help.
- Accommodations and Modifications: Ensure the school is willing to provide necessary accommodations, like extended test time and use of assistive technology.
- Extracurricular Activities: Opportunities for social integration and confidence building.
- Peer Support Programs: Mentoring and tutoring programs to provide additional support.

High Schools

As Ava entered high school, her parents focused on finding a school that offered both academic rigor and strong support services. They selected a school with a comprehensive learning support center and a reputation for accommodating students with learning differences. The school provided regular workshops on study skills and time management, which were particularly helpful for Ava.

Key Considerations:

- Learning Support Centers: Availability of centers that offer tutoring, study skills workshops, and test accommodations.
- College Preparatory Programs: Schools that prepare students for the demands of higher education.
- Technology Integration: Access to assistive technologies and software that aid learning.
- Inclusive Environment: A school culture that embraces diversity and supports students with learning differences.
- Guidance Counseling: Strong guidance counseling services to help with course selection and college planning.

College Choices: Finding Supportive Environments

Emma, a high school senior with dyslexia, was determined to find a college that would support her academic needs. She visited several campuses and focused on schools with comprehensive disability services offices. She chose a university that offered extended exam time, note-taking services, and access to assistive technology. The school also had a supportive community and various student organizations for individuals with learning differences.

Key Considerations:

- Disability Services Office: A strong office that provides accommodations, support services, and advocacy.

- Academic Support Programs: Availability of tutoring centers, writing centers, and study skills workshops.

- Assistive Technology: Access to technologies such as text-to-speech software, speech-to-text software, and audiobooks.

- Flexible Learning Options: Schools that offer online courses, recorded lectures, and other flexible learning options.

- Supportive Community: Student organizations and support groups for individuals with learning differences.

- Admissions Policies: Schools that understand and support students with learning differences through their admissions process.

Transitioning: Tips for Smooth Transitions Between Educational Stages

Transitioning from Elementary to Middle School

Mia's parents and teachers collaborated to ensure a smooth transition from elementary to middle school. They held a series of meetings to discuss Mia's IEP and how her needs would be met in the new environment. Mia was given a tour of her new school and met her teachers before the school year started. Her new teachers were briefed on her learning profile and the strategies that had been effective in elementary school.

Tips:

- Early Planning: Begin discussions and planning well before the transition.
- School Tours: Arrange visits to the new school to familiarize the student with the environment.
- IEP Meetings: Hold transition IEP meetings to ensure continuity of support.
- Teacher Collaboration: Ensure communication between current and future teachers about effective strategies and accommodations.
- Student Involvement: Involve the student in the planning process to address their concerns and preferences.

Transitioning from Middle to High School

Ethan's middle school support team worked closely with his high school to ensure a smooth transition. They updated his IEP to reflect the increased demands of high school and provided training for Ethan on using organizational tools and study strategies. Ethan also attended a summer program at his new high school, which helped him acclimate to the new environment and meet some of his future classmates.

Tips:

- Update IEPs: Reflect the academic and organizational skills needed for high school.

- Skill Development: Focus on developing study skills, time management, and self-advocacy.

- Summer Programs: Enroll in transition programs or summer camps offered by the high school.

- Peer Connections: Facilitate early connections with peers through clubs or orientation activities.

- Parental Support: Encourage ongoing parental involvement and communication with the school.

Transitioning from High School to College

Ava's high school provided her with resources to help her transition to college. She attended workshops on self-advocacy and managing accommodations. Ava's parents helped her connect with the disability services office at her chosen college, where she registered for accommodations and learned about the available support resources. She also joined a summer bridge program that introduced her to college-level coursework and campus life.

Tips:

- Self-Advocacy: Teach students to advocate for their needs and seek accommodations.

- Connect with Disability Services: Register with the college's disability services office before the semester starts.

- Orientation Programs: Participate in orientation and bridge programs to ease the transition.

- Support Networks: Establish connections with support groups and peer mentors on campus.

- Organizational Skills: Continue to develop time management and organizational skills to handle increased academic demands.

CHAPTER 6

MODERN TEACHING STRATEGIES

Multi-Sensory Learning: Techniques and Benefits

Jake, a second-grader, struggled with reading and writing due to his dyslexia. His teacher, Ms. Garcia, decided to implement multi-sensory learning techniques to support him. This approach engaged multiple senses simultaneously, making learning more accessible and effective for Jake.

Techniques:

1. Visual Aids: Ms. Garcia used colorful letter cards, charts, and diagrams to help Jake visualize letters and words. She also incorporated picture books and graphic organizers.

2. Auditory Elements: Jake's lessons included songs and rhymes to teach phonics and spelling rules. Ms. Garcia used read-aloud sessions to model fluent reading and helped Jake practice with phonetic games and auditory exercises.

3. Tactile Activities: Jake traced letters in sand, used clay to form letters, and employed textured letters to enhance his tactile learning experience.

4. Kinesthetic Learning: Incorporating movement, Ms. Garcia had Jake use body movements to form letters and words, hop on letter mats, and participate in interactive games that involved physical activity.

Benefits:

- Enhanced Memory and Recall: Engaging multiple senses helped Jake better retain information and recall it more easily.

- Improved Engagement: The variety of activities kept Jake motivated and interested in learning.

- Holistic Learning Experience: Multi-sensory learning catered to Jake's unique learning style, addressing his specific needs.

Studies show that multi-sensory learning techniques significantly improve reading skills in dyslexic students, making it a highly effective approach for literacy instruction (Multi-Sensory Learning and Literacy Development, 2022).

Structured Literacy: Evidence-Based Approaches

Emma, a fifth-grader with dyslexia, found reading and writing tasks overwhelming. Her school adopted a structured literacy approach to support students like Emma. This evidence-based method provided explicit, systematic instruction in foundational literacy skills.

Approaches:

1. phonological Awareness: Emma's lessons included exercises to develop her ability to recognize and manipulate sounds in words. Activities such as segmenting and blending sounds helped her understand the building blocks of language.

2. Phonics: Emma received direct instruction in phonics, learning the relationships between letters and sounds. Her teacher used a sequential program that started with simple sounds and gradually introduced more complex patterns.

3. Fluency: To build reading fluency, Emma practiced reading passages aloud with guidance. Her teacher provided feedback and used repeated readings to improve her speed and accuracy.

4. Vocabulary: Emma's vocabulary lessons focused on teaching the meanings of new words, using context clues, and word analysis strategies.

5. Comprehension: Emma learned strategies to improve her reading comprehension, such as summarizing texts, predicting outcomes, and making inferences. Her teacher used graphic organizers to help Emma organize and understand information.

Benefits:

- Systematic Progression: Structured literacy provided a clear, systematic progression of skills, building a strong foundation for Emma's reading and writing abilities.
- Explicit Instruction: The explicit nature of the instruction ensured Emma received clear, direct teaching of each literacy component.
- Skill Integration: By integrating phonological awareness, phonics, fluency, vocabulary, and comprehension, structured literacy addressed all aspects of Emma's reading development.

Structured literacy approaches are highly effective for students with dyslexia, as they provide a comprehensive, systematic method for teaching reading and writing skills (Structured Literacy and Reading Achievement, 2021).

Classroom Accommodations: Tools to Help Dyslexic Students Succeed

Alex, a high school junior, faced significant challenges with reading and writing due to his dyslexia. His teachers implemented various classroom accommodations to support his learning and help him succeed academically.

Accommodations:

1. **Extended Time:** Alex was given extra time on tests and assignments, allowing him to process information and complete tasks without feeling rushed.

2. **Assistive Technology:** Alex used text-to-speech software to help with reading assignments and speech-to-text tools for writing tasks. These technologies enabled him to access information and express his ideas more effectively.

3. **Note-Taking Support:** Alex received copies of class notes and was allowed to use a recording device during lectures to review the material later.

4. **Modified Assignments:** His teachers provided alternative assignments that accommodated his learning needs, such as oral presentations instead of written reports and allowing graphic organizers instead of traditional outlines.

5. Quiet Testing Environment: Alex was allowed to take tests in a separate, quiet room to minimize distractions and help him focus.

Benefits:

- Reduced Stress: The accommodations reduced Alex's stress and anxiety, allowing him to perform to the best of his abilities.
- Increased Accessibility: Assistive technologies and modified assignments made learning more accessible for Alex.
- Enhanced Performance: With the right support, Alex was able to demonstrate his knowledge and skills more accurately.

Classroom accommodations play a crucial role in helping students with dyslexia succeed. These tools and strategies provide the necessary support to overcome learning barriers and achieve academic success (Classroom Accommodations and Student Performance, 2023).

These stories and research findings illustrate the importance of modern teaching strategies, such as multi-sensory learning, structured literacy, and classroom accommodations, in supporting dyslexic students and helping them succeed academically.

CHAPTER 7

THE DIGITAL REVOLUTION

Assistive Technology: Tools and Apps That Support Learning

Ethan, a middle school student with dyslexia, struggled with reading and writing tasks. His parents and teachers explored various assistive technologies to support his learning.

Tools and Apps:

1. Text-to-Speech Software:

- Example: Kurzweil 3000
- Function: Converts written text into spoken words, allowing Ethan to listen to his reading assignments.
- Benefit: This tool helped Ethan comprehend texts better and keep up with his coursework.

2. Speech-to-Text Tools:

- Example: Dragon NaturallySpeaking
- Function: Converts spoken words into written text, enabling Ethan to complete writing assignments more easily.

- Benefit: It allowed Ethan to express his ideas without the hindrance of his writing difficulties.

3. Audiobooks:

- Example: Audible, Learning Ally
- Function: Provides audio versions of books, which Ethan could listen to instead of reading.
- Benefit: Audiobooks made literature more accessible to Ethan and helped him enjoy reading.

4. Word Prediction Software:

- Example: Co:Writer
- Function: Suggests words as Ethan types, helping with spelling and sentence structure.
- Benefit: This tool improved Ethan's writing fluency and reduced frustration.

5. Reading Pens:

- Example: C-Pen Reader
- Function: Scans text and reads it aloud, providing immediate support for difficult words or passages.

- Benefit: The reading pen was a portable solution that Ethan could use in various learning environments.

These tools transformed Ethan's learning experience, making reading and writing tasks more manageable and boosting his confidence. He began to participate more actively in class and enjoyed learning again.

Digital Resources: Online Courses and E-Books

Mia, a high school student with dyslexia, found traditional textbooks challenging. Her school introduced her to various digital resources to enhance her learning experience.

Online Courses:

Khan Academy

- Function: Provides free online courses in various subjects, featuring video lessons and interactive exercises.
- Benefit: Mia used Khan Academy to supplement her classroom learning, accessing visual and auditory explanations that made complex concepts easier to understand.

Coursera

- Function: Offers online courses from universities and organizations worldwide.
- Benefit: Mia enrolled in courses related to her interests, benefiting from flexible learning schedules and diverse instructional methods.

E-Books:

Kindle, Apple Books

- Function: Digital books that can be read on various devices, often with adjustable text sizes and background colors.
- Benefit: Mia used e-books to customize her reading experience, reducing eye strain and enhancing readability.

OverDrive

- Function: Provides access to digital libraries, allowing users to borrow ebooks and audiobooks from their local libraries.
- Benefit: Mia could access a wide range of reading materials without cost, enriching her learning and leisure reading.

Digital resources provided Mia with alternative ways to engage with content, improving her understanding and retention. She excelled in her studies and developed a love for lifelong learning.

Success Stories: How Technology Has Changed Lives

Alex, a college student with dyslexia, faced significant challenges in higher education. However, with the help of technology, he achieved remarkable success.

Assistive Technology:

Text-to-Speech and Speech-to-Text:

Read Write

- Function: Provided both text-to-speech and speech-to-text functionalities.

- Benefit: This comprehensive tool supported Alex in both reading and writing tasks, ensuring he could handle complex academic texts and express his ideas effectively.

Organization Tools:

Evernote, OneNote

- Function: Digital note-taking and organization apps that allow users to create, store, and organize notes.

- Benefit: Alex used these apps to keep his notes organized, set reminders, and manage his study schedule.

Digital Resources:

Online Research Databases:

JSTOR, Google Scholar

- Function: Provides access to academic papers, articles, and research materials.

- Benefit: Alex could conduct research more efficiently, accessing a wealth of information online.

Educational Platforms:

LinkedIn Learning

- Function: Offers online courses in various professional and technical skills.
- Benefit: Alex took courses to enhance his skills and prepare for his career, benefiting from the flexibility and variety of topics available.

With the support of technology, Alex was able to navigate the demands of college successfully. He graduated with honors and secured a job in his desired field, attributing much of his success to the tools that helped him overcome his dyslexia.

Emma's Professional Growth

Emma, a professional with dyslexia, leveraged technology to excel in her career.

Assistive Technology:

Productivity Tools:

Grammarly

- Function: Provides real-time grammar and spell-checking, along with writing style suggestions.

- Benefit: Emma used Grammarly to ensure her written communications were clear and error-free.

Communication Tools:

Zoom, Slack

- Function: Facilitates video conferencing and team communication.

- Benefit: These tools enabled Emma to participate actively in team meetings and collaborate effectively with colleagues, regardless of her reading and writing challenges.

Digital Resources:

Professional Development Platforms:

Skillshare

- Function: Offers courses and workshops on various skills and topics.

- Benefit: Emma took courses to improve her professional skills and stay current with industry trends.

E-Books and Audiobooks:

Audible for Business

- Function: Provides access to audiobooks on leadership, management, and other professional development topics.
- Benefit: Emma listened to audiobooks during her commute, continuously learning and growing in her career.

Technology played a crucial role in Emma's professional development. She advanced rapidly in her career, becoming a valued team leader and mentor, thanks to the tools that helped her manage her dyslexia effectively.

CHAPTER 8

BRAIN STRENGTHENING EXERCISES

Sam, a bright seven-year-old with dyslexia, struggled with reading and writing. His parents learned about brain plasticity, the brain's ability to reorganize itself by forming new neural connections throughout life. This concept gave them hope that Sam's brain could adapt and improve with targeted exercises.

Brain Plasticity:

Definition: Brain plasticity, also known as neuroplasticity, is the brain's remarkable ability to change and adapt as a result of experience. This means that through practice and learning, the brain can develop new pathways and strengthen existing ones, enhancing cognitive functions.

Mechanisms: Neuroplasticity involves the growth of new neurons (neurogenesis), the formation of new synapses (synaptogenesis), and the strengthening of existing synapses through repetitive activity.

Relevance to Dyslexia: Research shows that individuals with dyslexia can benefit from brain plasticity. By engaging in specific exercises, they can improve their reading and comprehension skills, making it easier to overcome learning challenges.

Studies on brain plasticity have demonstrated that targeted interventions and exercises can lead to significant improvements in reading skills for dyslexic individuals (Neuroplasticity and Dyslexia, 2022).

Specific Exercises: Activities to Enhance Reading and Comprehension Skills

Lily, a nine-year-old with dyslexia, began a program of brain-strengthening exercises designed to enhance her reading and comprehension skills. Her mother, Mrs. Thompson, worked with her daily, using a variety of activities to stimulate Lily's brain.

Phonological Awareness Exercises:

1. Rhyming Games:

- Activity: Playing rhyming games where Lily had to identify and generate words that rhyme.
- Benefit: Improved Lily's ability to recognize and produce rhyming words, which is crucial for phonological awareness.

2. Sound Segmentation:

- Activity: Breaking down words into individual sounds (e.g., "cat" becomes /k/ /a/ /t/) and blending sounds to form words.
- Benefit: Enhanced Lily's ability to decode words by recognizing their phonemic structure.

Memory and Sequencing Exercises:

1. Memory Card Games:

- Activity: Playing memory card games where Lily had to match pairs of cards with similar sounds or images.
- Benefit: Strengthened Lily's working memory and visual memory, important for reading and spelling.

2. Story Sequencing:

- Activity: Arranging picture cards in the correct sequence to tell a story.
- Benefit: Improved Lily's ability to understand and recall the sequence of events, aiding in reading comprehension.

Visual and Auditory Processing Exercises:

1. Eye-Tracking Activities:

- Activity: Practicing eye-tracking exercises where Lily followed moving objects with her eyes.
- Benefit: Enhanced Lily's visual processing skills, making it easier for her to follow lines of text.

2. Auditory Discrimination Games:

- Activity: Playing games that required Lily to differentiate between similar sounds (e.g., "bat" vs. "pat").
- Benefit: Improved Lily's auditory processing abilities, crucial for distinguishing between similar-sounding words.

Comprehension and Vocabulary Building Exercises:

1. Interactive Read-Aloud:

- Activity: Reading books aloud together and discussing the story, asking questions, and predicting outcomes.
- Benefit: Enhanced Lily's comprehension and vocabulary through interactive and engaging reading sessions.

2. Word Maps:

- Activity: Creating word maps where Lily wrote a new word in the center and added related words, synonyms, and definitions around it.
- Benefit: Helped Lily expand her vocabulary and deepen her understanding of word meanings.

Engaging in a variety of targeted exercises can significantly enhance the reading and comprehension skills of dyslexic individuals by promoting brain plasticity and strengthening neural pathways (Reading Interventions and Neuroplasticity, 2021).

Implementing Exercises: Creating a Daily Routine for Children

Jamie, a ten-year-old with dyslexia, needed a structured routine to practice his brain-strengthening exercises consistently. His parents, Mr. and Mrs. Parker, collaborated with his teacher to create a daily routine that fit into Jamie's schedule.

Daily Routine:

1. Morning Session:

- Activity: Phonological Awareness Exercises

- Duration: 15 minutes

- Details: Jamie and his parents played rhyming games and practiced sound segmentation activities before school. This helped kick-start his brain and prepare him for the day's learning.

2. After-School Session:

- Activity: Memory and Sequencing Exercises

- Duration: 20 minutes

- Details: After returning home from school, Jamie played memory card games and arranged story sequencing cards. These activities reinforced his memory and sequencing skills, making it easier for him to follow and understand classroom instructions.

3. Evening Session:

- Activity: Visual and Auditory Processing Exercises

- Duration: 15 minutes

- Details: In the evening, Jamie practiced eye-tracking exercises and auditory discrimination games. These exercises helped him improve his visual and auditory processing skills, essential for reading fluency.

4. Bedtime Routine:

- Activity: Comprehension and Vocabulary Building

- Duration: 20 minutes

- Details: Before bed, Jamie and his parents engaged in interactive read-alouds and created word maps. This routine not only enhanced Jamie's comprehension and vocabulary but also fostered a love for reading.

Weekly Review:

- Activity: Progress Tracking

- Duration: 30 minutes (once a week)

- Details: Every weekend, Jamie's parents reviewed his progress with him, discussing the exercises he enjoyed and the improvements he noticed. They also adjusted the routine based on his evolving needs and preferences.

This structured routine helped Jamie develop a consistent practice of brain-strengthening exercises. Over time, he showed significant improvement in his reading and comprehension skills, gaining confidence and enjoying learning more.

Creating a structured routine for brain-strengthening exercises ensures consistency and maximizes the benefits of neuroplasticity, leading to significant improvements in cognitive and academic skills for dyslexic individuals (Structured Interventions and Cognitive Development, 2020).

CHAPTER 9

BECOMING BETTER READERS: A HOME PROGRAM

Structured Home Program: Step-by-Step Guide

Sophia, an eight-year-old with dyslexia, found reading challenging and often frustrating. Her parents decided to implement a structured home reading program to support her development. Here's a step-by-step guide based on their approach:

Step 1: Assess Current Reading Level

- Objective: Determine Sophia's current reading abilities to tailor the program to her needs.
- Activity: Use simple reading assessments or seek input from her teacher. Identify strengths and areas needing improvement, focusing on phonics, fluency, and comprehension.

Step 2: Set Clear Goals

- Objective: Establish specific, achievable goals to monitor progress.
- Activity: Set short-term goals (e.g., recognizing sight words) and long-term goals (e.g., reading a short book independently). Write these down and review regularly.

Step 3: Create a Reading Schedule

- Objective: Develop a consistent reading routine.

- Activity: Allocate dedicated reading time each day, such as 20 minutes in the morning and 20 minutes before bed. Ensure this schedule is flexible but consistent to form a habit.

Step 4: Choose Appropriate Reading Materials

- Objective: Select books that match Sophia's reading level and interests.

- Activity: Use leveled readers, decodable books, and picture books. Incorporate her interests (e.g., animals, fairy tales) to make reading engaging.

Step 5: Incorporate Multi-Sensory Learning

- Objective: Enhance reading through multi-sensory techniques.

- Activity: Use visual aids (flashcards), auditory activities (songs, rhymes), and tactile exercises (tracing letters in sand). Combine these methods to reinforce learning.

Step 6: Track Progress and Adjust as Needed

- Objective: Monitor Sophia's progress and adapt the program accordingly.

- Activity: Keep a reading log, noting books read, time spent, and any improvements. Adjust goals and activities based on her development.

Structured home programs with clear goals and consistent routines significantly improve reading skills in dyslexic children (Home-Based Reading Interventions, 2021).

Interactive Activities: Games and Exercises that Make Reading Fun

Max, a seven-year-old with dyslexia, thrived on interactive and playful learning. His parents incorporated games and exercises into his reading routine to make it enjoyable.

Phonics and Word Recognition Games:

1. Word Bingo:

- Activity: Create bingo cards with sight words or phonics patterns. Max covers the words as they are called out.

- Benefit: Reinforces word recognition and phonics skills through a fun, competitive game.

2. Flashcard Hunt:

- Activity: Hide flashcards with letters or words around the house. Max finds and reads each card aloud.

- Benefit: Combines physical activity with reading practice, making learning dynamic and engaging.

Comprehension and Sequencing Activities:

1. Story Cubes:

- Activity: Use dice with pictures or words to create a story. Max rolls the dice and constructs a narrative based on the images or words.
- Benefit: Enhances creativity, storytelling, and comprehension skills.

2. Picture Sequence:

- Activity: Arrange picture cards in the correct order to tell a story. Max describes each step of the sequence.
- Benefit: Develops understanding of story structure and sequencing.

Vocabulary and Spelling Games:

1. Word Ladder:

- Activity: Start with a simple word (e.g., "cat") and change one letter at a time to form new words (e.g., "cat" to "bat" to "bet").
- Benefit: Improves spelling, phonics, and vocabulary.

2. Alphabet Soup:

- Activity: Create a "soup" with magnetic letters. Max picks letters to form words related to a theme (e.g., animals, food).

- Benefit: Enhances letter recognition and vocabulary through thematic play.

Interactive Reading Apps:

1. Starfall:

- Activity: Use the Starfall app for interactive reading games and phonics activities.

- Benefit: Provides engaging, educational content tailored to Max's reading level.

2. Epic

- Activity: Explore a vast library of e-books, audiobooks, and interactive stories.

- Benefit: Offers a variety of reading materials, making reading fun and accessible.

Interactive activities and games enhance motivation and engagement, leading to improved reading skills in dyslexic children (Interactive Learning and Literacy, 2020).

Parental Involvement: How Parents Can Support Their Children

Olivia, a nine-year-old with dyslexia, benefited immensely from her parents' active involvement in her reading journey.

Creating a Positive Reading Environment:

- Objective: Make reading a positive, stress-free activity.

- Activity: Set up a cozy reading nook with comfortable seating, good lighting, and a variety of books. Celebrate small achievements and make reading a fun, family activity.

Modeling Good Reading Habits:

- Objective: Demonstrate the importance and enjoyment of reading.
- Activity: Read regularly in front of Olivia, discussing favorite books and sharing stories. Make reading a part of daily life, such as reading recipes, signs, or menus together.

Providing Encouragement and Praise:

- Objective: Build Olivia's confidence and motivation.
- Activity: Offer specific praise for her efforts and progress. Celebrate milestones, such as finishing a book or mastering a difficult word. Encourage a growth mindset by focusing on effort and improvement rather than perfection.

Collaborating with Teachers and Specialists:

- Objective: Ensure consistent support across home and school environments.
- Activity: Communicate regularly with Olivia's teachers and any specialists involved in her education. Share insights and strategies, and implement recommended practices at home.

Using Assistive Technology:

- Objective: Enhance Olivia's reading experience through technology.

- Activity: Utilize text-to-speech apps, audiobooks, and reading apps tailored for dyslexic learners. Encourage Olivia to explore these tools and integrate them into her daily routine.

Staying Informed and Educated:

- Objective: Keep up-to-date with best practices and resources for supporting dyslexia.

- Activity: Read books, attend workshops, and join support groups for parents of dyslexic children. Stay informed about new research, tools, and strategies to better support Olivia's learning journey.

Active parental involvement is crucial in supporting dyslexic children's reading development, leading to significant improvements in their skills and confidence (Parental Involvement and Dyslexia, 2019).

CHAPTER 10

INSPIRING STORIES OF SUCCESS

Dyslexia, often perceived as a stumbling block, can actually be a springboard to greatness. Many successful individuals have navigated the challenges of dyslexia, turning their unique cognitive traits into strengths. Their stories of perseverance, innovation, and triumph serve as powerful reminders that dyslexia does not limit potential—it redefines it. Here, we explore the lives of men, women, and young adults who have achieved remarkable success despite their dyslexia. We also delve into the common strategies they employed, the motivations that drove them, and the invaluable lessons learned from their journeys.

Profiles of Successful Dyslexics

Richard Branson: Entrepreneur and Philanthropist

Richard Branson, the flamboyant founder of the Virgin Group, is a prime example of how dyslexia can be harnessed to achieve extraordinary success. Branson struggled with traditional schooling, finding it difficult to read and write. His dyslexia made academic subjects challenging, but it also fueled his creative thinking and risk-taking spirit. Branson's unconventional approach to business, characterized by his ability to see the big picture and think outside the box, has led to the creation of over 400 companies under the Virgin brand. His story illustrates how embracing dyslexia can lead to innovative solutions and groundbreaking achievements.

Whoopi Goldberg: Actress, Comedian, and Activist

Whoopi Goldberg's journey from a struggling student to an Emmy, Grammy, Oscar, and Tony award-winning performer is nothing short of inspirational. Goldberg was often mislabeled as lazy or unintelligent due to her difficulty with reading and writing. It wasn't until later in life that she was diagnosed with dyslexia. Despite the challenges, Goldberg's natural talent and determination propelled her to stardom. Her ability to connect with audiences through humor and storytelling has made her a beloved figure in entertainment. Goldberg's success story emphasizes the importance of recognizing and nurturing talent beyond traditional academic measures.

Steven Spielberg: Director and Filmmaker

Steven Spielberg, one of the most influential filmmakers in history, struggled with dyslexia well into his career. Spielberg faced significant challenges in school, often feeling isolated and misunderstood. However, his dyslexia did not hinder his creative genius. Spielberg's unique way of seeing the world has translated into some of the most iconic films of all time, including "E.T.," "Jurassic Park," and "Schindler's List." His ability to visualize and bring complex stories to life on screen is a testament to how dyslexia can enhance creative capabilities. Spielberg's journey underscores the power of perseverance and the importance of following one's passion.

Agatha Christie: Renowned Author

Agatha Christie, known as the "Queen of Mystery," wrote 66 detective novels, 14 short story collections, and the world's longest-running play, "The Mousetrap." Christie's dyslexia made writing a painstaking process, with spelling and grammar posing significant hurdles. Yet, she developed a distinctive writing style that captivated millions of readers worldwide. Christie's meticulous plotting and keen understanding of human nature turned her dyslexia from a disadvantage into a hallmark of her storytelling. Her legacy highlights how determination and creativity can transform perceived weaknesses into defining strengths.

Bella Thorne: Actress and Advocate

Bella Thorne, a young actress and singer, has become a vocal advocate for dyslexia awareness. Diagnosed at a young age, Thorne faced bullying and low self-esteem due to her reading difficulties. With the support of her family and educators, she developed coping strategies that allowed her to excel in her career. Thorne uses her platform to inspire other dyslexic individuals, emphasizing the importance of self-acceptance and resilience. Her advocacy work aims to break the stigma surrounding dyslexia and empower young people to pursue their dreams regardless of their learning differences.

Overcoming Obstacles: Common Strategies and Motivations

1. Leveraging Strengths:

  - Many successful dyslexics focus on their strengths rather than their weaknesses. Richard Branson, for instance, capitalized on his big-picture thinking and ability to innovate, which were assets in his entrepreneurial endeavors. Identifying and nurturing one's strengths can lead to a fulfilling and successful career.

2. Seeking Support:

  - Building a support network of understanding family, friends, and mentors is crucial. Whoopi Goldberg credits her mother for her unwavering support and encouragement. Support systems provide emotional strength and practical assistance, helping individuals navigate their challenges effectively.

3. Adopting Assistive Technology:

  - Technology can be a game-changer for dyslexic individuals. Steven Spielberg utilized various tools to aid his reading and writing, allowing him to focus on his creative pursuits. Modern assistive technologies, such as speech-to-text software and audiobooks, can significantly enhance productivity and learning.

4. Developing Resilience:

  - Overcoming dyslexia often requires developing a strong sense of resilience. Bella Thorne's journey from a bullied student to a successful actress demonstrates the power of resilience.

Building resilience involves learning from setbacks, maintaining a positive outlook, and continually pushing forward despite difficulties.

5. Embracing Creativity:

- Dyslexic individuals often possess exceptional creative abilities. Agatha Christie's unique approach to storytelling and plot development is a testament to this. Embracing and cultivating creativity can lead to innovative solutions and extraordinary achievements.

Lessons Learned: Key Takeaways from Their Journeys

1. Dyslexia is a Different Way of Thinking:

- Dyslexia should not be viewed as a deficit but as a different cognitive approach that can offer unique advantages. The ability to think outside the box, visualize solutions, and approach problems creatively are common traits among successful dyslexics.

2. Early Diagnosis and Intervention Matter:

- Early identification and support can make a significant difference. Providing dyslexic individuals with the tools and strategies they need from a young age helps them build confidence and succeed academically and professionally.

3. Persistence and Determination are Crucial:

- The stories of Richard Branson, Whoopi Goldberg, and others highlight the importance of persistence. Achieving success often requires overcoming numerous obstacles and maintaining determination in the face of adversity.

4. Support Systems are Vital:

- Whether it's family, friends, mentors, or professional networks, having a strong support system is essential. These networks provide the emotional and practical support needed to navigate the challenges of dyslexia.

5. Advocacy and Awareness Make a Difference:

- Raising awareness about dyslexia and advocating for supportive environments can help break down barriers. Bella Thorne's advocacy work has inspired many and contributed to a more inclusive understanding of dyslexia.

6. Celebrate Diversity:

- Dyslexic individuals bring valuable diversity to the table. Their unique perspectives and approaches can lead to innovative ideas and solutions that benefit society as a whole.

CHAPTER 11

MOVING FORWARD: A POSITIVE OUTLOOK

Julia was diagnosed with dyslexia in elementary school. Initially, she struggled with low self-esteem and felt different from her peers. Her journey towards self-acceptance began when she attended a summer camp for dyslexic children. There, she met other kids with similar challenges and discovered her own strengths.

Building Self-Confidence:

1. Recognizing Strengths:

- Activity: At the camp, Julia participated in various activities like art, drama, and sports, where she excelled and received positive feedback.
- Outcome: She realized that her dyslexia did not define her abilities and that she had unique talents to offer.

2. Positive Reinforcement:

- Activity: Counselors at the camp emphasized positive reinforcement, celebrating small victories and improvements.
- Outcome: Julia's confidence grew as she started to believe in her own potential.

3. Role Models:

- Activity: Julia learned about successful individuals with dyslexia, such as Richard Branson and Agatha Christie.

- Outcome: These role models inspired her to pursue her dreams and not be limited by her dyslexia.

Developing Resilience:

1. Facing Challenges:

- Activity: Julia faced various challenges during her school years, from difficult assignments to social pressures.

- Outcome: Each challenge taught her to be persistent and resilient, learning to overcome obstacles with determination.

2. Support Systems:

- Activity: Julia's family, teachers, and friends provided unwavering support, encouraging her to keep trying even when things were tough.

- Outcome: This support network helped her develop a strong sense of resilience and self-worth.

3. Self-Advocacy:

- Activity: Julia learned to advocate for herself, requesting accommodations and seeking help when needed.

- Outcome: By taking charge of her own learning and needs, she built a sense of empowerment and independence.

Building self-confidence and resilience is crucial for dyslexic individuals. Positive reinforcement, recognizing strengths, and supportive environments contribute significantly to their development (Self-Confidence and Dyslexia, 2020).

Future Trends: What's on the Horizon for Dyslexia Support

Advancements in technology and educational practices are opening new avenues for supporting dyslexic individuals. From early diagnosis to personalized learning tools, the future of dyslexia support looks promising.

Technological Innovations:

1. AI and Machine Learning:

- Development: AI-driven tools are being developed to provide personalized learning experiences. These tools can adapt to individual learning styles and provide tailored feedback.

- Example: Smart educational apps that adjust the difficulty level based on the user's progress, helping dyslexic students learn at their own pace.

2. Virtual Reality (VR) and Augmented Reality (AR):

- Development: VR and AR are being used to create immersive learning environments that engage multiple senses.
- Example: VR simulations that help dyslexic students visualize and interact with concepts in a more intuitive way, enhancing comprehension and retention.

3. Speech Recognition Technology:

- Development: Improved speech recognition software aids in reading and writing tasks, converting spoken words into text and vice versa.
- Example: Applications like Dragon NaturallySpeaking and Google Voice Typing that help dyslexic individuals with writing and note-taking.

Educational Trends:

1. Universal Design for Learning (UDL):

- Development: UDL principles advocate for flexible learning environments that accommodate diverse learning needs.

- Example: Classrooms equipped with multiple means of representation, expression, and engagement to support all students, including those with dyslexia.

2. Early Screening and Intervention:

- Development: Advances in screening tools allow for earlier identification of dyslexia, leading to timely and effective interventions.

- Example: Programs like DIBELS (Dynamic Indicators of Basic Early Literacy Skills) that help teachers identify at-risk students in kindergarten and first grade.

3. Collaborative Learning Models:

- Development: Emphasis on collaborative and inclusive learning environments where students work together and support each other.

- Example: Peer tutoring programs and group projects that foster a sense of community and shared learning.

Future trends in dyslexia support focus on personalized, technology-driven solutions and inclusive educational practices that cater to diverse learning needs (Future of Dyslexia Support, 2021).

Final Thoughts: Encouragement and Hope for Readers

Encouragement:

1. Believe in Yourself:

- Message: Sarah emphasizes the importance of self-belief. "Your dyslexia does not define you. Believe in your abilities and never give up on your dreams."

- Outcome: Her self-confidence grew as she embraced her strengths and pursued her passions.

2. Seek Support:

- Message: "Don't hesitate to ask for help. There are many people who want to see you succeed."

- Outcome: With the support of her community, Sarah was able to access resources and accommodations that made a significant difference in her education.

3. Stay Resilient:

- Message: "Challenges are part of the journey. Stay resilient and keep pushing forward."

- Outcome: Sarah's resilience helped her overcome setbacks and achieve her goals.

Hope:

1. You Are Not Alone:

- Message: "There are many people with dyslexia who have achieved great things. You are not alone in this journey."

- Outcome: Knowing that others have faced similar challenges and succeeded can be a powerful source of motivation.

2. The Future is Bright:

- Message: "With advancements in technology and education, the future for dyslexic individuals is full of possibilities."

Outcome: Sarah is optimistic about the opportunities that lie ahead for herself and others with dyslexia.

3. Celebrate Your Achievements:

- Message: "Every achievement, no matter how small, is a step forward. Celebrate your progress and be proud of your journey."
- Outcome: Celebrating her achievements helped Sarah stay motivated and focused on her goals.

Encouragement and a positive outlook are crucial for dyslexic individuals. Supportive environments and a belief in one's potential contribute significantly to success and well-being (Positive Outlook and Dyslexia, 2022).

CONCLUSION

Dyslexia Resolve: A Comprehensive Guide to Understanding, Managing, and Thriving with Dyslexia" is a beacon of knowledge and hope for anyone touched by dyslexia. As we conclude this journey through the intricate landscape of dyslexia, it becomes clear that what many perceive as a learning disability can, in fact, be a powerful asset when properly understood and managed.

Throughout this book, we have demystified dyslexia, exploring its neurological foundations and dispelling common myths. We've emphasized the critical importance of early detection and intervention, equipping parents and educators with the tools they need to identify and support dyslexic children from the earliest stages. By providing evidence-based educational strategies, we have shown how multi-sensory learning and structured literacy can transform the learning experience for dyslexic students.

Technology has emerged as a game-changer in this field, and we have highlighted the myriad ways in which digital tools and resources can empower dyslexic individuals. From assistive technology to online courses, these innovations offer new pathways to learning and success.

Personal stories of successful dyslexic individuals have illustrated that dyslexia does not limit potential—it redefines it. These narratives of triumph over adversity, coupled with practical strategies and common motivations, serve as powerful reminders that resilience, creativity, and determination can overcome any challenge.

We have also addressed the lifelong journey of dyslexia, recognizing that challenges evolve but can be managed at every stage of life. From childhood and adolescence through adulthood, dyslexic individuals face unique hurdles, yet they also develop unique strengths.

Parents, educators, and dyslexic individuals themselves will find in these pages not just a guide, but a source of inspiration and encouragement. We have provided practical home programs, tips for parental involvement, and strategies for building self-confidence and resilience.

Looking to the future, we have explored emerging trends and innovations that promise to further enhance dyslexia support. The landscape of dyslexia is continually evolving, and staying informed about the latest research and technologies is crucial.

In conclusion, "Dyslexia Resolve" is more than a resource—it's a call to action. It's an invitation to embrace dyslexia as a unique perspective that enriches our world. By fostering understanding, providing support, and celebrating the strengths of dyslexic individuals, we can create a society where everyone has the opportunity to thrive.

Whether you are a parent, educator, dyslexic individual, or advocate, your role in this collective effort is invaluable. Together, we can unlock the potential within every dyslexic mind, turning challenges into triumphs and dreams into realities.

APPENDICES

Resource List: Books, Websites, and Organizations

Books

1. "Overcoming Dyslexia" by Sally Shaywitz

2. "The Dyslexia Empowerment Plan" by Ben Foss

3. "Dyslexia Advocate! How to Advocate for a Child with Dyslexia within the Public Education System" by Kelli Sandman-Hurley

Websites

1. International Dyslexia Association (IDA)

   URL: dyslexiaida.org

2. Understood

   URL: [understood.org](https://www.understood.org)

3. DyslexiaHelp at the University of Michigan

   URL: dyslexiahelp.umich.edu

Organizations

1. The Yale Center for Dyslexia & Creativity

2. Decoding Dyslexia

3. Learning Disabilities Association of America (LDA)

Glossary of Terms: Key Terminology Explained

1. Dyslexia: A specific learning disability characterized by difficulties with accurate and/or fluent word recognition and by poor spelling and decoding abilities.

2. Phonemic Awareness: The ability to hear, identify, and manipulate individual sounds (phonemes) in spoken words, a critical skill for reading development.

3. Phonics: A method of teaching reading based on the sound of letters, groups of letters, and syllables.

Further Reading: Recommended Academic and Popular Literature

Academic Literature:

1. "The Dyslexic Advantage: Unlocking the Hidden Potential of the Dyslexic Brain" by Brock Eide and Fernette Eide

2. "Dyslexia: Theory and Practice of Remedial Instruction" by George Pavlidis

3. "Understanding Dyslexia: A Guide for Teachers and Parents" by Denis Lawrence

Popular Literature:

1. "Fish in a Tree" by Lynda Mullaly Hunt

2. "Thank You, Mr. Falker" by Patricia Polacco

3. "The Dyslexic Advantage: Unlocking the Hidden Potential of the Dyslexic Brain" by Brock Eide

and Fernette Eide

REFERENCE

1. Classroom Accommodations and Student Performance (2023)
2. Early Identification and Intervention for Dyslexia: A Review of the Evidence (2023)
3. Future of Dyslexia Support: Innovations and Trends (2021)
4. Home-Based Reading Interventions: Effective Strategies for Dyslexic Learners (2021)Reading Interventions and Neuroplasticity: A Meta-Analysis (2021
5. Interactive Learning and Literacy: The Role of Games and Activities (2020)
6. Multisensory Approaches to Early Literacy Instruction (2019)
7. Multi-Sensory Learning and Literacy Development (2022)
8. Neuroplasticity and Dyslexia: Unlocking the Brain's Potential (2022)
9. Neuroscientific Insights into Early Reading Development (2021)
10. Parental Involvement and Dyslexia: Best Practices for Support (2019)
11. Reading Interventions and Neuroplasticity: A Meta-Analysis (2021
12. Self-Confidence and Dyslexia: Building Strength Through Support (2020)
13. Structured Interventions and Cognitive Development in Dyslexic Children (2020)
14. Structured Literacy and Reading Achievement (2021)
15. The Impact of Early Screening on Reading Outcomes (2022)The Impact of Early Screening on Reading Outcomes (2022)
16. The Role of Genetics in Dyslexia (2021)